Selected Pages From The Diary Of An Indoor Cat

Selected Pages From The Diary Of An Indoor Cat

W.R. Runyan
Editor

Order this book online at www.trafford.com
or email orders@trafford.com

Most Trafford titles are also available at major online book retailers.

Printed in the United States of America.

ISBN: 978-1-4269-6886-0 (sc)

Trafford rev. 05/12/2011

www.trafford.com

North America & international
toll-free: 1 888 232 4444 (USA & Canada)
phone: 250 383 6864 • fax: 812 355 4082

Table of Contents

Acknowledgments x
From The Editor xi
Introduction 1
Cat-talk to English 1
Me 3
From An Alley Cat Back To A House Cat 5

Pages From The Diary 7
Diary, First Page 7
Me and The Snake 8
The Stupid Outdoor Cat 9
The Missing Entries 11

The Opossum Episode 12
Old Grandpa 13
Another Grandpa Story 14
The Fuzzy Family 15
The Story Of Yet Another Grandpa Cat 18

A West Texas Bobcat 19
A Joke (not original with me) 20
My First Trip To The Vet 21
Why Cats Don't Like Thunder 23
The Cat That Could, And Did 24

Outdoor Fuzzy (ODF) 25
The Pink Flamingos 27
The Cat From Missouri 28

Charlie	29
The Celebrity	30
The Night The Burglar Alarm Went Off	31
The Backyard Rabbits	32
The Bored Kitty	33
Training D	34
Training W	35
The Bathtub Cat	36
The Armadillo	37
Cat Rivalry	39
The Lizards	40
My Genealogy	42
Community Service	43
Locked In	44
Hiding	45
Early Cat History	46
Cat Related Words	47
Cat Breeds	49
Drooler's Rebuttal	50
Cat Coloration	51
The Squirrel That Nearly Wasn't	52
My Name	53
We Cats Can Count	54
Tossing Socks	55
The Cat Pole	56

A Snowy Day	59
Surprised	60
Trapped	61
My headache	62
The City Coyotes	63

Acknowledgments

This book would not have been possible had not my wife Delma tolerated THE cat for many years. She (Delma, not the cat) also provided all of the illustrations.

From The Editor

This collection of pages from the diary of an indoor cat was begun during a month that I spent in a rehab center. Doing this was certainly a lot more interesting than spending my time moving up and down the rehab halls in a wheelchair. It should be noted that as near as I can tell, these diary entries are more or less true, although some may have been embellished more than others. Since I had access to D's collection of cat photographs and sketches, and with the agreement of THE cat, some of those photographs and sketches have been interspersed with the chosen diary pages.

Because of the cat's unfamiliarity with the English language and the limitations of my computer program, the punctuation in this diary is somewhat questionable. However, in the interest of authenticity, the publisher has decided to leave the punctuation as it is.

The Editor
Dallas, Texas, 2011

Introduction

Editor's Note: For the introduction to her diary, I persuaded the cat to compile these additional pages.

Cat talk to English

I suppose that one thing that should be discussed early on is how my cat thoughts have been transcribed into human readable words. In the beginning I gave considerable thought to that problem. First was the requirement to somehow convert my very complex thoughts into something humans could understand. The next problem was to figure out how to transfer those understandable thoughts to the human brain. Archie the cockroach solved the cockroach to human information transfer problem by learning to spell English and then laboriously typing his messages by diving headfirst onto individual typewriter keys. It finally occurred to me, being a relatively intelligent cat, that the way to go was to sit next to someone working at a computer and just transfer my thoughts to them and let them and the computer software convert my thoughts to readable English.

An earlier house cat

This picture inspired the method used to produce the text of this manuscript

Me

For the introduction, perhaps a bit about my background (THE cat) is in order. I am a shorthaired black-and-white house cat (not one of those low class barn cats) with a pattern design called, I believe, tuxedo. The household I started life in treated me kindly, fed me well, and admonished me to never, never go outside. Being, I suppose, a fairly normal house cat, I would dart out at any opportunity. One day during a lot of activity, with many people coming and going about the house, I didn't have to dart out, I just wandered out, and since no one seemed to notice, I thought I would do a little neighborhood exploring. I didn't pay much attention to the time, and late in the day I thought I could hear some "here kitty, here kitty" calls. Even though some of them began to sound a bit frantic, as cats are prone to do, I paid no attention. It was a hot day and eventually I began to think a nice saucer of milk would hit the spot. So back to the house I went and did some scratching on the screen door. This should have led to a quick opening of the door and a "wherever have you been" comment. But this time, nothing. No worry, the lady of the house has likely just gone to the grocery store and the man of the house is still at work. I was sort of tired from all of my explorations and curled up at the back door and went to sleep. When I awoke it was dark and there was no light on in the house. Whoops! The next morning there was still no sign of anyone in the house. Over the next few days I found out the activity had been the movers taking the furniture out of the house, and the frantic "kitty" calls I faintly heard and ignored were just before the man and lady of the house drove off to their new home. Thus began my few months as an **alley cat.**

5

From An Alley Cat Back To A House Cat

At first, being alone didn't bother me, but I soon began to be hungry and thought I better look into my options. My first hope was that some of the neighborhood cats that were fed outside would share their food. Boy, was I ever wrong! Then I considered birds. There were lots of them flitting about the yards and in the trees, but they sure flew fast. I finally managed to catch one but liking feathers must be an acquired taste. Next, I noticed a few little creatures around the alleys that were sort of predictable in their running habits. I caught some of them (mice) and they were pretty good eating. The next problem was the weather. When it rained there was generally a porch somewhere that would keep off the rain, but pretty soon it started getting cold at night and even with no rain it was uncomfortable. (Remember, I'm shorthaired.) At this point it seemed obvious that I had better find another home before it really got cold. I needed to look for a house with no dog, and preferably no cat(s). There was a house a few blocks away that seemed to be okay, except that the houses on either side had dogs, although one was very old and wobbly. One day a man was sitting on the back porch of the house looking somewhat bored so I walked by him and started purring. He picked me up and held me for a bit and then I left. The next day I stopped near the front door and started meowing piteously like I was starving (actually I felt sort of like I was). The lady of the house came out and left some food. Then I rolled over on my back and tried to look helpless. She reached down and scratched my stomach and smiled. So far so good. The next morning I went in search of a nice fat mouse. After finding and catching a suitable one, I took it to the front porch and carefully positioned it in the middle of a rug by the door. Sometime during the day, the mouse disappeared, and the next morning there was a fresh plate of food on the porch. Shortly after that I was no longer an alley cat.

THE Cat

Pages From The Diary

Diary, page 1

Since I am starting a diary rather late in life, I rather suspect that a lot of the pages will be reminisces instead of day-to-day happenings. While this may not be the way diaries are usually kept, remember that this is my diary.

Me and The Snake

One day an outside door was open a crack so I took advantage of the opportunity and darted out. I quickly ran around to the offside of the house where I couldn't be so easily found and brought back in. (I don't know why people have such a fetish about cats staying indoors.) Anyway, as I was walking around I noticed a black stick a few feet long lying on the ground. As I walked past it one end suddenly rose up and went whizzing by my head (only my quick response kept it from hitting me in the face). As the "head" of the stick went by I saw a tongue and two sharp looking teeth. After consulting my extensive hereditary databank I concluded within seconds that the stick was really what people call a snake, and that those long teeth were quite likely poisonous! I reached down and caught the snake's tail in my teeth and yanked. Then, being half off the ground, it couldn't move along anymore, and furthermore couldn't turn around and bite me. It was sort of fun yanking it up, dropping it, and then as it got all set to glide away, snatch it up again. That snake didn't have much stamina, and after a few minutes it just lay quietly on the ground. It wasn't much fun so I just ate the whole thing (except for the head and teeth). It really was not as good as the cat food I get indoor.

The Stupid Outdoor Cat

Occasionally, I saw an outdoor cat come up to the back door looking for food handouts. However, this cat's elevator (and it does hurt me to say something derogatory about another feline) just doesn't seem to go to the top. Anyway, a few days of observation on its part would show that it is only at mealtimes that there is anyone in the room with the back door. Those mealtimes are only at a few predictable times each day (humans seem to lead very predictable and structured lives) and yet that cat will show up randomly throughout the day and meow pitifully for a food hand out, even though it is quite fat and rotund! I have tried to explain the daily routine to it by talking through the screen door during mild days when the main door is open, but all it does is roll over on its back and start purring. I don't know whether it was just not listening to my clear and simple discussion, no big words (cat words of course) nor complicated sentence structures, or whether it is even dumber than I have suspected.

It also would rather be petted than eat, not surprising I suppose, considering how fat it is. Still, it shows no sign of understanding the old adage of "don't bite the hand that feeds you." Several times, when it didn't get the petting it felt like it deserved, it bit and/or scratched D.

That of course, led to reduced feedings and pettings and I had to then listen (through the screen door) to a series of tirades concerning how stingy D was compared to the people at that stupid cat's home. I suggested that he might try staying home where things were so great, but the next day he showed up again at an odd hour during a fairly heavy rain-oh well.

11

The Missing Entries

I don't know why I didn't realize this earlier, but with the way the diary pages are produced (see **Cat Talk To English**) I can't make any entries unless the computer is on and being used. Some times W spends a bit of every day at the computer, but then there are times when he may not use it for days on end. This month it was something over a week that the computer was not on but the only thing that happened worth mentioning during that time was that I got shut up in a closet overnight. I missed my evening cat nibbles but I wasn't very hungry anyway. What was a bit of a problem though was not having access to my sandbox.

The Opossum Episode (This didn't involve me, I'm just the scribe.)

One of those mentally challenged outdoor (feral) cats looked like it was a candidate for spaying, so one winter day D decided to trap it and take it to the vet. First there was the problem of finding a suitable trap, and then there was the problem of enticing the stray cat in to it. (Actually, that cat had a lot of street smarts and wasn't as dumb as I thought). Anyway, one evening two or three days later, D looked at the trap and said "ah hah, success." So before daylight the next morning, D loaded the "cat" and trap into the car and was waiting at the vet's door when he opened. Fortunately, D looked in the trunk to see how the cat was faring and realized that it was really an opossum! She made a hasty retreat back home and dumped a very irate half-grown opossum.

13

Old Grandpa

He was not really, at least I don't think, my grandpa, but he was old and very smart in the way of birds. For example, some afternoons he would lie sprawled out in the backyard looking just like a very dead cat. Mockingbirds, not terribly bright but very curious (sort of like a cat with no brain), would land on the ground near the cat and gradually edge closer and closer. Old grandpa would just lie there, not twitching a muscle nor blinking an eye until one of those birds got a little too close. Then grandpa would sort of explode and have himself a nice afternoon snack.

Another Grandpa Story

Old grandpa cat stayed with a next-door neighbor, so when they were moving away, it seemed reasonable for them to take grandpa cat along. W, who considered that he knew a bit about such things, having moved his first set of cats in a gunnysack when he was seven years old, offered his help. The neighbor declined any help, saying he had a nice cardboard box to put old grandpa in. A few hours later, the neighbor showed up at our back door with scratches and blood from his fingernails to his elbows. He said that since old grandpa spent about as much time in W and D's back yard as it did in his, why didn't W and D just keep him, which they did. It didn't make much difference because it's hard to tell seven outdoor cats from six.

The Fuzzy Family

(Note: none of this family is to be confused with the dumb outdoor cat of an earlier entry).

This particular story is before my time but I accessed it from W's mind (actually not very difficult). W and D were walking around the neighborhood one weekend and stopped to look at a house under construction. No one was working on the weekend, but there was a half grown longhaired kitty there. It was tame, plump, and apparently well fed from the carpenter's lunch scraps. However, softhearted D picked it up and carried it home, saying it needed looking after. She set it on the porch, and left W to watch it while she went to the grocery store for some cat food. When she came back, no cat! It was gone, and stayed gone. Then, some months later W saw a cat wandering in the backyard that looked sort of like a grown up version of the lost kitty. Some time later that cat showed up with three kittens in tow. Up close, the mother cat sure looked to both W and D like they thought the grown-up kitten would have looked, except that this one had short hair and was wild. Anyway, D felt obligated to feed both the mother cat and her three kittens.

Little Fuzzy, while a very likable kitty, was though, a bit marginal in brains. As an example

of his antics, a somewhat older yard cat was a pretty good hunter and was quietly creeping up on an unsuspecting bird when Little Fuzzy, just a kitten at the time, saw the stalking cat, but probably not the bird, (or perhaps he didn't know what it was) and went jumping through the grass and of course scared away the bird. Unforgiving, the older cat gave him a fierce clout on an ear.

Grumpy (the only female) was the smallest cat of the litter, but also as might be judged by the name, the most ill tempered. When her eyes were just barely open and her mother first brought the kittens to the house, W went out on the porch, started to pet her, and promptly drew back a bloody finger. Later, when much older, Grumpy took over the task of keeping the yard free of stray cats. She was never very big, but her speed and temperament were always sufficient to discourage even the largest intruder.

Outdoor Fuzzy (the one remaining outdoors after the other two became house cats), wasn't fuzzy at all, was by far the largest of the Fuzzy family, and also probably the best hunter of the family. It was not unusual for him to catch a bird and bring it to the back porch for W and D to admire. As he was bringing it back he could generally be heard meowing as loud as was possible with a mouthful of flapping bird*. As an aside, shortly after the mother cat with the three kittens showed up, W was walking around the block and saw a cat in a front yard that looked much like the mother cat <u>except</u> that it was longhaired and seemed very friendly. That cat had shown up there as a kitten about the time the longhaired kitten disappeared from W's house.

---

*Editor's note: there is an entry entirely devoted to Outdoor Fuzzy later on.

The Story Of Yet Another Grandpa Cat

I never knew this cat; the story came out of the computer one day as I was idly accessing W's brain.

One day, a long time ago, W was sitting on the back porch of another house feeling sort of blue when a big old yellow tomcat jumped into his lap and started purring very loudly. W had never seen the cat before, but it turned out that new neighbors had just moved next door. The cat, called "Carrot" belonged to their little girl, and the cat and girl were very attached to each other. When the little girl was in her room and the cat was outside, he could usually be found lying on the brick ledge that was at the bottom of her window.

W didn't particularly like the name Carrot, and occasionally just called out "here cat, here cat", and oddly enough, the old yellow tom responded. (Actually, the name Carrot also seems to me like a pretty stupid name for any cat, whether he is yellow, blue, or green. It sort of makes me wonder whether the cat had a mental problem and the name "Carrot" was a nice way of saying the cat behaved more like a vegetable.) As time went on, if the cat were in the neighbor's house, and the little girl heard W calling "here cat", she would open the door and Carrot would dash out and over to wherever W was calling from!

A West Texas Bobcat

(Note: this story was related by a Dallas attorney and is, therefore suspect. Nevertheless, I thought it was worth repeating.)

Two teenage boys out in West Texas caught a bobcat and puzzled for a while about what to do with it. They then decided to put it in a suitcase (see "Another Grandpa Story" for a discussion of the problem of putting a cat in a container). Having done that they then wrapped several turns of rope around the suitcase to make sure it wouldn't come open unintentionally. They next carried the suitcase out to the only highway through town and set it down by the side of the road. Later, a car came by, the people in it decided there might be something of value in the suitcase and stopped long enough to pick it up and put it in the car. A little further down the road (just long enough for the suitcase to be opened) there was a great squealing of tires, the car stopped, and the occupants and one irate bobcat came sailing out.

A Joke (not original with me)

One day a yard cat had an accident and lost a good portion of its tail. As the owner was putting it in the car to take it somewhere, a neighbor inquired as to which vet he was taking it. The owner said he wasn't going to a vet, he was going to WalMart. Why WalMart, inquired the neighbor. "Because they are the biggest retailer in the country."

My First Trip To The Vet

The day started off just like any other but then I noticed a strange contraption setting on the dining room table. My, I thought, what are they eating today that requires a peculiar looking bowl like that? Exercising my usual curiosity, I hopped up on the table, a no-no itself, and closely examine the "bowl." Oddly, it appeared to have a handle on the top, a door on one side and one of W's old shirts crumpled up on the bottom. Oh well, it doesn't involve me, so I wandered off and forgot all about it.

An hour or so later D picked me up, started petting me profusely and gently telling me what a fine cat I was (and of course that was something that I already knew). She walked toward the dining room table (of fine tiger striped oak, which for some reason that I never understood, W and D always called the "green" table). As she passed the table she suddenly pushed me through the door of the bowl and clanged it shut. Up until then I had free run of anywhere in the house and now I was in what I decided was a "cage", and a very small one at that. Next, I was carried outdoors to a car (I'd never been in one before, although during my "alley cat" days I had learned to keep them from running over me). The car then moved away, but not fast enough to confuse my internal global positioning mechanism. I certainly didn't intend to be hauled off and dumped where I couldn't find my way back home.

I probably shouldn't have worried about that happening, but some shady acquaintances from my alley cat days had told me of cats being taken miles away and tossed out. I also yelled a lot just to let D know I didn't appreciate this kind of treatment. Anyway, I wound up, not abandoned in a far away field, but in veterinarian's (a vet's) office where a kindly looking man jabbed me a few times with a big needle, patted me on the head, said I was a "good kitty" and sent me home. Since I could tell that we were indeed going toward home, I didn't meow on the way back, just slept.

Why Cats Don't Like Thunder

Actually, for all I know, most cats may revel in a good thunder and lightning storm. Further, on reflection, I don't know why thunder (but not the lightning) scares the wits out of me.

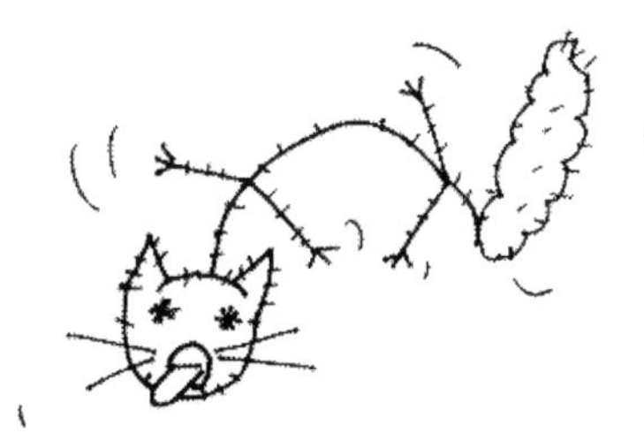

The Cat That Could, And Did!

In the not be too dim past, people with indoor cats thought nothing of scooping them up, whisking them off to a veterinarian, and having the cats front claws yanked out. W and D had a friend with such a cat (see "Charlie" for more on him), which in its youth liked very much to claw the furniture and climb the drapes. I personally never knew, but always suspected that these pastimes had something to do with the eventual claw removal. Anyway, Charlie really liked to climb drapes, and after his front paws stopped hurting he started to go shinnying up the curtains on the front window. Of course, after his initial leap he came sliding back to the floor and landed with a loud plop. As Charlie found out, it's awfully hard to hang on to a drape without claws or toeholds. Now, some cats might have been a bit discouraged, but not Charlie. He sat on the floor awhile, considered what resources he had (back claws and a mouth full of teeth). After a few false starts he found out that he could climb those drapes quite handily with teeth and rear claws. I have no idea what his owner thought about teeth marks in her fancy drapes.

Outdoor fuzzy (ODF)

Why W and D call him "Fuzzy" was a mystery to me. His hair was short, straight, and glossy. No sign of fuzz anywhere. Perhaps the most remarkable thing about ODF was that even though D always fed him, and W never did, if she called, the cat would never come, but if W called and the cat could hear him and was not trapped, he would come at a lope. He did, unfortunately get trapped a lot in the church buildings down the road. If he didn't show up for his evening meal W would go down to the church buildings and wander around calling "here Fuzzy" until he heard him meow and then, usually, get him out. I'll bet it looked and sounded funny for a grown man to be wandering around an empty church calling "here Fuzzy!" One of the evenings when the cat was trapped in a locked church building room and W couldn't get him out, D call the pastor and asked if he would come back to the church and let the cat out. "No, I can't be bothered" was answer. After D reminded him of the mess and smell a trapped cat could produce overnight, ODF was free and home in less than 30 minutes! Sometimes that cat would come up to the French doors that opened from the outside to the study, look in, and if D were working at the computer, walk away, but if W were there he would meow loudly to be let in. Then, after getting in, if W didn't pay him enough attention he would unsheath his rather large claws, reach up to a bare arm hovering over the computer and scratch, leading to many a bloody arm. This always seemed to me like poor treatment to someone that had saved his hide many times, but W tolerated it.

The Pink Flamingos

Even though now I am a dyed in the wool house cat with little inclination to dash outside (except maybe for a few blades of grass), I do find it interesting to look out a window at the wildlife. One morning there was something new and just a bit unfriendly. Almost touching the window were several big ugly birds on very long spindly legs. Their necks were also long, curved, and terminated with heads that had the most peculiar looking big black beaks that turned down at the end. And to top it off they were all mostly pink. I jumped at them a few times even though there was a big pane of glass between us. I also hissed a few times, but they seemed oblivious to everything. Ugly and dumb, I thought. Then I overheard D and W talking and realized those things in the window were plastic flamingos. Gosh, who was dumb???

The Cat From Missouri

(This story is from one of D's sisters)

One evening, D's sister and a friend were sitting on her front porch when a car driving by stopped suddenly, the driver got out, raised the hood, picked up something from the engine compartment and flung it down by the side of the road. Curiosity consumed the sister and her friend, so as the car drove off, they went to see what had been thrown down. It was a kitten with badly burned paws from having stood on the hot exhaust manifold of the car engine. Apparently its curiosity caused it to climb up into the engine compartment while the car was parked in the driveway.

After a trip to the vet and a few weeks rehabilitation the kitten pretty much recovered and apparently decided it wanted to live permanently with D's sister. It couldn't find any mice as a present, but each night it did line up some of its toys at the side of the sister's bed and presumably lived there happily ever after.

Charlie

Charlie started out as a barn cat and was actually before my time. This information has been gathered by listening to W and D. When D first saw Charlie he was a scrawny little kitten living on an Oklahoma farm. She felt sorry for him and took him home with her. As he grew up (a yellow tom), he didn't fit in well with the other cats that W and D had so D gave him to an old lady who was retired but had worked for years for a veterinarian. That lady became very attached to Charlie and when she moved to Florida she took him (still a young cat) with her. The lady died a few years later and had requested that Charlie be returned to D. The lady had also been in correspondence with her old employer the vet, and he had agreed that if D would look after Charlie, he would provide free vet service. (Speaking for myself, I think that could be way too much vet attention.) Anyway, D agreed to take Charlie back, so one day he arrived at the airport after having flown from Florida first-class in a box under the seat of a Florida veterinarian. Talk about preferred treatment, I think most of us would have been stuffed in some sort of cage and traveled in the baggage compartment!

The Celebrity

I'm a celebrity! At least I think so. It all started when I was up on a bathroom lavatory looking around. I thought I heard something in the wall, and to get a better look, I scratched off some of D's nice wallpaper. Underneath it I saw a bunch of little wormlike creatures busy chewing up the wall. About then D came in, saw what I had done and called W. Uh oh, I thought, I'm in some kind of bad trouble. However W took one look at the torn wallpaper and the mess of "worms" underneath, picked me up and said "good kitty". There is just no predicting what these humans will do.

That afternoon some man came and sprayed a lot of foul-smelling stuff around the house, petted me, and ask D for my picture. More and more confusing. It turned out that the "worms" were actually termites, which eat wood and left alone can literally eat enough wood to cause a house to collapse, and I, THE cat, had found them before any serious damage was done. My picture was posted on the bulletin board in the office of the company that came out to eliminate the termites. A cat spotting the termites was so unusual that I think someone wrote a short article about it in the exterminating company's newsletter and included my picture in it.

The Night The Burglar Alarm Went Off.

In the middle of the night (yes it was dark, but no, it was not stormy) the home burglar alarm went off and I nearly jumped out of my skin. I must admit though that it was sort of funny to see W padding about the house barefooted with a flashlight in one hand and a 45 revolver in the other. Eventually he and the alarm company together figured out that a motion detector in the garage had tripped but that the door from the garage to the house had not been opened. By then the police were there and could see no sign of the outdoor garage door having been opened.

What happened was that big Outdoor Fuzzy, the one who kept getting trapped in the church buildings, had slipped unnoticed into the garage and remained there until he decided to climb a ladder propped up in one corner of the garage. (Cats do like to climb ladders!) The sensitivity of the motion detector had been adjusted to overlook small animals like cats, but to trip when a person entered the garage. Unfortunately, the sensor was located near the ceiling in the corner of the garage where the ladder was setting. Thus, when Outdoor Fuzzy got to the top of the ladder his face was right next to the detector, and of course it tripped!

The Backyard Rabbits

As I looked out the window yesterday there were two young rabbits playing and chasing each other. Mostly the playing was just like I would've expected, but one time, when they were separated by several feet, one stopped dead still and the other started running toward it at top speed. I was spellbound, wondering if either of them were going to blink or if there were shortly going to be two dead rabbits laying in the yard. However, just before the collision, the one that had stopped jumped straight up in the air and the other, which never slowed and never swerved, ran right under him.

The Bored Kitty

D has a sister with a somewhat lonesome young cat (hardly more than a kitten). It would like to be chasing and catching things like mice but such creatures are absolutely not to be found in the sister's house. There may be an occasional water moccasin but no mice (this sister lives in Louisiana next to a bayou). Anyway, as a substitute for pouncing on a real live mouse, the kitten will pick up one of its toys, halfway hide it, walk away, then turn around, run to the toy, and fiercely attack it. I'll bet the Chinese-made fake fur of the toy doesn't smell or taste anything like a mouse. I can sort of sympathizers with that kitty because there aren't any mice to catch in this house either. What can be done though, is to swat at the occasional fly that makes its way in the house, or catch and eat the crickets that sometimes come in, although they aren't nearly as entertaining as a cornered mouse, and they certainly aren't as good to eat.

Training D

I heard W tell D that in discussions with some psychologist acquaintance, the training of children came up and it was the psychologist's contention that not only did parents train their children, but the children, starting almost from the time they were born, trained their parents. For example, the parents learn to interpret the baby's cries so they can tell whether it is hungry or its diaper needs changing. That started me to thinking about the different things I have trained D to do. Some of which, I might add, were not easy. I can now get her to feed me when I'm hungry and to follow me to my place of choice as to where to put down the food. It was pretty hard, but I was also able to convince her to get up several times during a night to put out food when hunger pangs struck me. It took quite a number of nights meowing in her ear and pulling the covers from over her eyes before she would do that. However, she sure wasn't very enthusiastic. People seem to like to sleep uninterrupted for hours at a time. They just don't comprehend catnaps.

Training W

Actually, there has been no training of W. He is hardheaded, determined, obstinate, obtuse, inflexible, stubborn, pertinacious, and ϒ♣δΘℵ. (I don't know how to translate that last word into English, and that is probably just as well.)

The Bathtub Cat

This entry doesn't involve any of my acquaintances, and didn't even happen in my lifetime, but it seems so interesting that I am going to repeat the story. It seems that D's mother once had a cat (ill tempered, but that's not part of this story) that liked to play in the family bathtub when there was no water in it. The cat would lie down on its side with its back against the inside of the tub and then used its back feet to propel itself around and around the inside of the tub. I'm not quite sure how it did that but I think it must have kicked the end of the tub each time it went around.

The Armadillo

One day when the front door was open I looked out through the screen and saw W apparently walking a small strange looking animal. Eventually, after D took some photographs, W came back in the house and tossed the little creature onto the couch. I wouldn't have liked that, and I was surprised that W would do such a thing. Even though I didn't know what kind of animal it was, I decided that I was just as big as it was and if it tried anything I could probably whip it. So, with the idea of being sociable, I jumped up on the couch with it. It didn't so much as flick an eyelid. It also didn't seem to have a distinctive odor. In fact, it smelled pretty much like the couch. After a gentle pat of a paw, it still didn't move. Then, a closer examination showed that the little animal was not alive at all, and was made of cloth. I later found out that it was supposed to look like an armadillo and that W's brother had given it to him as a joke.

Cat Rivalry

D's daughter has two grown cats from the same litter. One of them likes to curl up in a lavatory and sleep, probably because the lavatory is cool. The other cat apparently doesn't care at all about sleeping there, but is cantankerous enough to sometimes beat the other one to the lavatory of choice and keep it out. This is the same cat that is said to have so terrorized a small puppy that even though the puppy is now grown, the cat still has the dog completely under its thumb (oops, I meant paw).

The Lizards

Occasionally, on the outside of the window that I usually look through, I see a creature that according to what I found during my rummaging through W's brain, is called a lizard. Since it's on the other side of smell impervious glass, I can't tell what it smells like, but it sure looks like it would be fun to bat around. Further inputs from W tells me that it is a kind of lizard that if attacked, its rather long tail drops off as a distraction while the remainder of the lizard runs away to live another day and grow another tail.

Anyway, to continue. Last night I came across a somewhat different looking lizard on the floor in the house. Ah ha, I thought, here's my chance to examine one more closely, and perhaps even watch the tail drop off. It turned out that this particular kind of lizard (called a gecko) didn't jettison its tail, and furthermore was quite agile. It whipped up the wall before I even got close to it, and then as I tried to reach up, the thing actually walked across the ceiling. Better luck next time, I thought. This afternoon I spotted another one, sneaked up and caught it, but before I could do more than just sniff it, D grabbed it out of my mouth and carefully carried it outside and turned it loose.

ADDED LATER: I finally caught one of those geckos when D wasn't watching. They taste pretty good—sort of like chicken.

My Genealogy

I heard W talking to some friend of his about collecting information on ancestors. W commented that though he had trouble going back any further than his great grandpa, he had an acquaintance that had traced his ancestors back to a particular valley in Scotland (wherever that is) several hundred years ago. Tracking back my ancestors seemed like fun until I realized that I didn't even know whom my grandfather was, and if I did, it would only take me back a few years. Setting forth to gather a bit of a history of us cats seemed more practical, so whenever W is susceptible, I will guide him to looking up and sharing some general cat history that might be in some of his books. Therefore, expect from time to time to see some entries on that subject.

Community Service

Yes, dear diary, I really did do some community service today. At first, the day looked routine, but then D picked me up and quickly slipped a sort of harness on me and started leading me around the house with a leash attached to the harness. Then we went outside and she put me in the car and off we went. At first, I thought we were going to the vet. With my excellent sense of direction, I soon realized that we weren't going there. Oh well, I thought, she has just changed vets, but that wasn't it either. The car turned in to the parking lot of a nursing home. D picked me up and carried me inside. We did some wending around and ended up in a room that contained a little furniture and a longtime acquaintance of W's and D's that was no longer able to live at home. This woman did like cats though, and D had taken me there so the woman could see and pet me. The petting was gentle and with the leash and harness, I couldn't have run away had I wanted to. Anyway, the lady certainly enjoyed it and I was glad to have been of help.

Locked In

This entry describes a happening of one of D's nephews and his cat. I am describing the episode here to help remind me not to get myself trapped in an automobile in this way (or any other). The nephew had a pet cat, and when going on long automobile trips (those of several hundred miles) he would usually take the cat along with him in his pickup. On one such trip the nephew stopped to look at something along the road and left the cat in the pickup with the doors shut and the windows rolled up. He was not going to be out of the car for more than five minutes so he didn't think the heat would be a problem for the cat.

When the nephew started to get back in the pickup he found that the door was locked and the keys were not in his pocket but still in the ignition lock. The cat, being curious about what was going on, and probably also a bit unhappy about being shut up, had stood up on his hind legs, put his front paws on the bottom of the car door window and looked out. While doing that, one of his paws had apparently rested on the switch that locked both doors, and pressed it down. After pondering the situation for a while, the nephew picked up a large rock from the side of the road and broke out one of the windows. There were also some rather loud words said that the cat didn't understand.

Hiding

If you are an indoor cat, it is great fun to hide from the people of the house. It is surprising how many obscure places there are in a house and how few of them people know about. It is also surprising how often one can set in a perfectly open spot and watch the owner peering into all kinds of out-of-the-way (to them) dark places. Of course, one must remember to change hiding places occasionally because even with their inferior memories, eventually the people of the house may remember where they last found you.

Early Cat History

This is a first of the entries of my version of cat genealogy, or perhaps I should say cat heritage. Cats are carnivorous and part of the family Felidae, which also includes tigers and lions. The cat form (with tails to help with balance, specialized claws, and teeth adapted to primarily eating small animals) apparently appeared about seven million years ago. Our claws really are pretty good for most purposes, but they don't work worth a flip if we start to go down a tree. They don't hold in that direction so we either just have to run down the tree or else jump. The cat in its present form seems to date back several thousand years to Egypt, and was domesticated by 1500 BC. Domesticated cats were present in Greece and in China by 500 BC and in India by 100 BC. They were in England by at least 900 AD and in the United States by 1750 AD.

Cat Related Words

I found out that the word "cat", combined with another word or two often means something quite afield from anything actually relating to a cat. I'm jotting down a few of those words to use when I'm conversing with some of those smart aleck outdoor cats that sometime come to the back door looking for a hand out.

Cat's paw Someone being used by another person to do something that they normally wouldn't do.

Cat's pajamas Some item or person that is very special.

Cat's back Used in the term "higher than a cat's back" and implying something excessively high, like a price.

Cat boat A sailboat with a particular kind of sail rigging.

Cat walk A walkway very high in the air with little support except at each end.

Top cat Top boss of an organization.

Fat cat Someone with lots of money or belongings.

Catnap A short nap.

Catty person Someone who make sarcastic comments about someone else, generally behind their back.

Catty wampus Some item that is severely out of alignment.

Catty cornered Some item, usually a structure that is not placed in alignment with surrounding items.

Cats and Jammer kids This entry really shouldn't be here. I've put it in my diary just to remind me of how us cats can go astray when trying to interpret the English language. The correct spelling is Katzenjammer Kids, which was the title of a comic strip popular in the 1930s.

Cat Breeds

More on cat genealogy. Dating back to my alley cat days, I thought there were four breeds of cats; house cats, yard cats, barn cats, and alley cats. Imagine my surprise to find that people have broken us up into many breed categories and that my four "breeds" are nowhere to be found. I don't think I'll try to put them all in my diary, just some that I want to remember. These are Siamese, Persian, Abyssinian, Burmese, Russian blue, and Domestic Short Hair. (I think the last one describes me).

Drooler's Rebuttal

First off, even though THE cat thinks I'm a pretty stupid member of the cat family, I managed to get this page included in her manuscript without her even knowing it. (Editor's comment: but I knew it.) I know my drooling is sort of disgusting but it is a malady I've had since childhood and the vets I have visited have not been able to do anything about it. They did say it isn't catching and that it certainly isn't a sign of early senility.

Just because I wasn't paying any attention, jumped up on a windowsill, and wound up spread eagled across some burglar bars doesn't mean I am bereft of common sense and judgment. Nor does the fact that I hung for two hours by one claw of each front paw that were caught in a sparrow trap indicate a lack of brainpower. That can happen to any cat that doesn't spend all of its time curled up in a rocking chair.

Cat Coloration

Everyone knows about black cats, white cats, and black and white cats. Yellow cats and gray cats also come to mind, along with blues (the color of the Russian Blue). Oddly enough though, W found no reference to any green cats! However, variations and combinations of the colors just listed provide enough different colors to boggle even my brain. Presumably to simplify things, many people, including W, just lump yellow cats, orange ones, and red ones into the broad category of yellow cats. Along with plain white there is cream, and silver. There are also grays and browns, as well as striped versions of most of the colors. Besides the hair being finer, under coatings generally have a somewhat different color than the overcoat. Then there is tortoise shell, with colors of black, orange, and cream; calico with the colors of black, red-orange, cream, and white; and several color combinations referred to as cameos, e.g. shell cameo, shaded cameo, smoke cameo, and tabby cameo. I'm glad I'm just a simple black-and-white cat, although it's sort of nice that my whiskers are so impressive (even if they aren't green).

The Squirrel That Nearly Wasn't

I don't particularly like the little critters, though in point of fact I've never actually eaten one. I probably won't either because I've been told that they can put up a pretty fierce battle. Anyway, the squirrel was out in the backyard wandering around in a lackadaisical fashion when all of a sudden a big fierce looking bird swooped down straight at the squirrel. I guess the squirrel heard something because it suddenly leaped to the backyard fence and the big bird (I later learned that people call it a red-tail hawk) had to give up the chase because it couldn't flap its big wings that close to the fence, and if it couldn't fly it certainly couldn't outrun the squirrel.

My name

Yesterday one of the outside cats wondered about how I got the name TC. Now that I have sort of recollected how it all happened I'm going to jot it down here so I don't forget it.

A few days after I had arrived, D commented that she thought I should have a name. W said that he didn't care what name as long as it wasn't something like snookums. About that time I came running down the stairs and started scratching on the side of the couch. W yelled out several things (in retrospect I think they were probably expletives) and ended up with the comment "that cat is a holy terror." He thought about it a bit and then said, "let's just call the cat Holy Terror." After a few more days it was changed to Terror Cat, or in short, Tarecat. When D took me to the veterinarian the first time, the receptionist wanted to know what my name was and then commented that Terror Cat was just not a good name for so sweet a cat, so she wrote down TC and that is what my name has been ever since. Actually, TC, Tarecat, or even Terror Cat is a better name than those of some of W and D's earlier cats, e.g. Grumpy and Drooler.

We Cats Can Count!

I heard W talking on the telephone (what an archaic form of communication) to some acquaintance of his and telling him that based on a recent observation, he surmised that I could count to at least two. That observation being that I saw two people who were visiting D and W drive away one morning, and then when the car came back later in the day and only one person got out of the car and came in, I kept going to the window and looking out, presumably for the second person. W interpreted this behavior as meaning I could count up to two. Good grief, if that were all, I couldn't even count the claws on one foot. Actually, we cats don't normally count very much; mainly we do trajectory calculations to plot a path when, for example, jumping from the top of the grandfather clock to the couch.

The fact that W was so impressed that I could actually count as far as two irritated me enough to consider biting him on the ankle. However, common sense took over at that point since I knew what would have happened next. As it is, I guess I'll just unburden myself on this diary page and W can read for himself my feelings when his computer spits out this page.

Tossing Socks

By standing up on my hind legs (I'm actually a rather long cat) I can just get my claws over the top of the top dresser drawer in W and D's bedroom. Today it (the drawer) was left not quite closed and I was able to reach up and pull the drawer open. I then hopped up into the drawer to see what was in it, and found a batch of W's socks. Socks are light and easily tossed about so I began burying in them and pitching a good number of them onto the floor. About that time D came in, took one look, began laughing, and picked me up out of the drawer. You know, I have the feeling that I won't see that drawer left open anymore.

The Cat Pole

Some time ago D came in with a strange looking thing that she indicated was for me to play on. It has two compartments stacked on top of each other that are big enough for me to crawl into. Then, on top of them is a pole with a sort of basket on the top that is big enough for me to curl up in. The whole thing is covered with something that looks like rug material that my claws sink into nicely when I'm climbing to the top. Anyway, one day I decided that since the top basket was no higher than D is tall, I could just as easily jump up to the top as to climb up over the compartments. My first attempt was catastrophic. I hit the basket and kept going - the whole thing toppled over with me. W was watching, saw what happened, and commented to D that the Cat Pole was another example of how things were made to look appealing to the buyer whether they would work or not. He said that he would fix it (W thinks he can fix anything) so it wouldn't tip over anymore when I jumped up on it.

Well, today he fixed it all right. I don't know whether it will tip over or not, but I do know I'm not getting close to it. I think he weighted it down with a whole bunch of wild animals that I don't want to have anything to do with. I can smell at least one dog, a stray cat or two, a snake, an opossum, and possibly a skunk. I also can't imagine how he crammed all those creatures into that one compartment.

Editor's note: W brought in several bricks from outdoors and stacked them in the bottom compartment to add weight and reduce the likelihood of the pole tipping over. Apparently all those animals had left their marks (odors) on the brick. Eventually the odors went away and THE cat then did enjoy the "pole."

A Snowy Day

Today was an interesting day. First, it snowed, which is a little unusual around here. Second, W and D had a fire going in the fireplace. Third, a bird flew into the window I usually look out of and fell to the ground. There is not anything particularly unusual about a bird hitting the window, but usually they can still fly away. Anyway, this bird knocked himself out cold. W went out and picked it up and brought it into the house. I was thinking it was nice of W to go out and bring in the bird for me, although I'm not particularly fond of them. But no, he didn't bring it in for me! He put it in a cardboard box and set the box down in front of the fireplace and covered the box was some sort of screen. While that flimsy screen would certainly keep the bird from flying out if it were functioning, such a screen was no match for me and I was preparing to knock it off and sample the bird when I saw the steely look on W's face and the rolled up newspaper in his hand. After thawing out for a while in front of the fire, the bird revived and began hopping about. W took the bird (a Junco, I think) back outside and it flew smartly away.

Surprised

This morning about daylight, while I was waiting for D to give me my breakfast, a strange looking beast stuck its long ugly snout (nose?) up against the window. The creature wasn't very big, not even as large as me, but I sure was glad that there was a double paned glass window between the two of us. About that time though, my superlative mental catalogue kicked in and told me that "it" was just a half grown possum (opossum to you language purists). Possums are not very smart, and though this one wanted to be friendly, we just couldn't communicate. No amount of ear wiggling, tail twitching, or any other body language seemed to be understood, and my meowing couldn't be heard through the glass, although I'm pretty sure he couldn't have understood any dialect of cat language anyway. Eventually, he just gave up and waddled away.

Trapped

Strange as it may sound, I locked myself in the bathroom this morning. D sometimes puts me in the bathroom when she has to prop the front door open for a bit. She did that this morning, and to sort of fight boredom I opened some of the drawers in the lavatory cabinet. There wasn't much of interest in any of them, but unfortunately, when one of the drawers was pulled out, the door to the bathroom would only open about an 1/8 inch. I'm not what you would call a fat cat, but I certainly couldn't squeeze out through that tiny crack. Anyway, after what seemed like hours, W came home, got a sharp pointed butcher knife, and by slipping it through the crack was able to jab the knife point into the side of the wooden drawer and gradually edge it closed and let me out.

My Headache

Have I got a headache! And it's all my fault. I probably shouldn't even discuss the happening, but maybe if I talk about it, it will make it easier for me to control myself and minimize future head knocks. It all started with a large flock of birds landing just outside the window. As I have commented before, I don't particularly like birds (for eating), but nevertheless, up close they do sort of excite me. So, with that big batch of birds right next to the window, I flattened my ears and started creeping up to the window. That was my hunter's instinct, I guess (which, I might add, served me well during my alley cat days). Something startled the birds, they started to fly away, and not seeming to be able to help myself I jumped --- into the window. A window may be thin, and it may be transparent, but it is, I can assure you dear diary, much harder than my head.

The City Coyotes

I thought I had some pretty scary experiences during my days as an alley cat but last night topped them all. About midnight (long after W and D had gone to bed) I was looking at the backyard from a living room window and admiring the bright moonlight when all of a sudden a pack of small ratty looking doglike creatures appeared. They ran up near the window, started yipping and yapping and finally broke into full-fledged howling. I moved back from the window and decided where to head for if they broke through the window and came into the house. That didn't happen, and the next morning W and D were talking about the coyotes they heard in the night. (It turns out that wolves, foxes, and coyotes are all part of the dog family so it wasn't unreasonable for me to think they were some sort of dogs.) D said that she had read in the newspaper that they killed cats (that's **me**) and had even attacked a small child somewhere in the city. W said he had grown up with the coyotes, regularly heard them howling at night, occasionally saw them in the pastures during the day, and always thought they were rather shy. (He must've grown up way out in the sticks somewhere!) Anyway, last night was the only time I have ever seen a coyote in my entire life, and with any luck, it will be the last time.